STOCK

AN ESSENTIAL GUIDE TO INVESTING IN THE STOCK
MARKET AND LEARNING THE SOPHISTICATED
INVESTOR MONEY MAKING SYSTEM

Descrierea CIP a Bibliotecii Naţionale a României

  Stocks. An Essential Guide To Investing In The Stock Market And Learning The Sophisticated Investor Money Making System. – Bucharest: My Ebook Publishing House, 2018
    ISBN 978-606-983-623-1

STOCKS

AN ESSENTIAL GUIDE TO INVESTING IN THE STOCK MARKET AND LEARNING THE SOPHISTICATED INVESTOR MONEY MAKING SYSTEM

My Ebook Publishing House
Bucharest, 2018

CONTENTS

INTRODUCTION

I want to thank you and congratulate you for downloading the book, "Stocks: An Essential Guide To Investing In The Stock Market And Learning The Sophisticated Investor Money Making System".

This book contains proven steps and strategies on how to mature in the art and practice of stocks investing. It essentially provides simple guides on what stocks entails (and does not entail). This is with the aim of putting you in a good position to offer advice on stock matters.

Lastly, you are sure to be equipped with useful information on the kind of stocks that suits an investors' preferences.

Thanks again for downloading this book. I hope you enjoy it!

CHAPTER 1

THE CONCEPT OF STOCKS
WHAT YOU SHOULD KNOW

Stocks are a kind of security. Basically, they secure something for you. That is, they secure some part of a firm's profit for you. Also, they secure ownership rights in part for you. They actually are a way to secure financial independence overtime.

The word "stocks" are quite popular these days. Many folks want to plunge their spare resources into one kind of stocks or another. Well, this is simply because, purchasing stocks is synonymous with purchase the assets of a firm, this time only a fraction of it.

You also can lay claim to such a firm's assets with the purchase of its shares. That sounds really cool, doesn't it? It feels good to partly own Deloitte or Ernst and Young or even Apple Inc. Maybe that's why stocks are so trendy these days.

Before I proceed, let me make this point crystal clear. Owning stocks do not mean you own the company. You only own shares of the company and not the company as a whole.

Owning stocks also means the firm or corporation in question is obliged to pay you dividends. That is, part of the profits it makes per business period accrue to the shareholders in such company.

I just said "shareholders." That would be deriving from shares, right? Do not be bothered, stocks and shares are literally the same thing. Only technically different.

You use stocks to refer to a conglomerate of shares. Shares, however, are used in reference to stocks held in a particular company.

In order words, when using the word "shares," it should be with a specific firm in view. For example, the proper thing would be to say, "I own shares in Apple" than to say, "I own stocks in Apple." This is especially when you don't have different kinds of shares in that company.

However, when stocks are used, they refer generally to the different shares owned in different companies. They could also mean diverse shares owned in a company. More like a common noun.

The number of stocks you own per unit of shares in a company, the more voting power you amass. Again, by voting power, you have a right to vote on who makes it to the board of directors.

Also, the more the unit of your shares, the more profits that accrue to you. Profits are paid on each unit of shares that you own. There are times, however, when these profits are not distributed but are retained. These are simply called "retained earnings."

Corporations withhold profits so as to grow the business thereby bringing about an increase in the value of its stocks.

The last thing to note about stocks are that they are equities. In order words, instead of using the word "shares", equities can be used as a replacement. This is so because it implies ownership of something.

By buying shares in a firm, you can legally lay claim to owning something. In this case, owning a fraction of a firm's earnings and assets.

It is important to note that equities are mostly used to refer to common stocks. We shall see the divisions in a bit. In order words, shares held by ordinary shareholders are typically called equities.

Stocks are also called equities because they are traded in the securities market. Recall that a share is a kind of security. It further establishes the fact that stocks are a kind of security that are traded. They are also called equity because they represent an ownership position. This ownership being only in part!

Who issues stocks?

The issuance of stocks is done by the company or corporation who wishes to raise capital. In order words, the need to raise capital to establish or grow a business is why companies issue out stocks.

Every well-meaning business venture desires to grow and expand in order to cater for more demand and make higher profits. It might even be that such a company wishes to open another outlet in a different city or location other than where it is currently based. This requires capital.

On the flip side, some group of people with innovative ideas decide to come together to set up a business. They need capital to set up. In both cases, the parties involved can decide to issue out shares to raise this capital rather than borrow it from the bank.

What stocks are not

You may have heard the term "bonds" and "bondholders" used before. Even if you haven't, I just mentioned it now (I chuckled a bit, pardon me).

Stocks are not bonds and should never be mistaken for bonds. When choosing what to invest in, stocks and bonds are very different options with different peculiarities. You'll be able to spot the difference shortly.

Those who hold bonds are called bondholders. Issuing bonds is an alternative way of raising capital other than issuing stocks. When it comes to bonds, the holders are viewed as creditors and treated so. They are not referred to as part owners and do not have any claim to the receipt of dividends.

Again, for emphasis, bondholders are treated by the corporation as creditors. What they receive in exchange for letting the firm have its money is called interest. This interest is often fixed. In order words, it does not appreciate or increase as the company makes more profits.

Also, at the end of the agreed period, the principal is repaid. The principal is the initial amount that the bondholder gave to the company in exchange for the bond certificate. This must be repaid. This is unlike shares that can be rolled over at the end of the agreed period.

Up to this point, it has been established that stocks are not bonds. They are quite different: With the ownership of bonds comes the entitlement to interest and your initial sum of money (principal) at the end of the agreed period.

Another clear thing is that bondholders are creditors; the company owes them. It, therefore, means that in the case where such company goes bankrupt, it has first to settle its bondholders. The reason is simple. The company is indebted to its creditors by law.

On the other hand, the shareholder who is a part owner has to wait for the creditors to be cleared before he receives his money back. This is just to point out the fact that legally, bondholders are given preference over shareholders as regards returns. This is the case especially when the company has need to fold up.

Another thing to note about what stocks is not is that it does not attract a fixed sum as returns. The amount you get as dividends today may be higher or lower than the previous return. This means that stocks do not guarantee a fixed amount as dividends.

The last feature worthy of note here is that stocks are not for the risk-averse investor. Very important to note! Why is this so? Well, because buying stocks comes with a risk. In order words, stocks are nothing near riskless investments.

You must not be fooled into thinking that purchasing stocks is risk-free; they are unlike bonds which are fairly risk-free. The idea that stocks make you part owner and not a creditor gives it away. As an owner in part, you may have to give up your investments if the creditors are yet to be settled.

The company, in extreme cases, may have to sell its assets to pay back what it owes the creditor. If that is done, it means the assets and earnings which are pooled from shareholders' funds all go into settlement of debt. The shareholder may be left with little or nothing to reclaim.

I hope it is quite evident already what stocks are in terms of definition and entitlements. I also hope that you understand what stocks are not in terms of what it cannot or does not confer. The concept of bonds should be a bit clearer by now as well.

With that settled, let us proceed, shall we?

CHAPTER 2

THE DIFFERENT TYPES OF STOCKS

Generally, there are two main types of stocks that a corporation or company can issue out. They are; common stock and preference stock.

Common stocks

Common stocks are as implied by the name, "common." This is true because when people mention stocks without placing an adjective before it, they usually are referring to common stock.

Stocks are called common when they firstly, confer voting rights. By voting rights, it means the holders of common stocks can participate in decision making of such company.

This way it works is this; a unit of share owned carries with it one vote. In other words, the more shares you own per unit, the greater voting rights you wield. The voting rights are used when there is need to select board members. They are otherwise called board of directors.

The board of directors are in charge of monitoring and affirming salient decisions made by the management of such company. Indirectly, therefore, common shareholders partake in deciding what happens in the firm.

Another thing to note about common stocks is that it promises a higher yield than those accruing to corporate bonds. These kinds of bonds have far more risk attached to it than the conventional government bond.

It means that even though corporate bonds gives a higher return on investment than government bonds, the returns to common stocks are even higher.

This is arguably so because of the higher risk attached to common stocks. So, you can safely say that with higher risks come higher returns and vice versa.

Still on risk matters, common stockholders risk losing all their investments in the liquidation crisis. We expect them to be the last to receive compensation when the company having their shares fold up.

The order in which the settlement takes place is thus; bondholders (we have seen why this is so already), then preference shareholders and then common shareholders.

Essentially, common shares are the most popular form in which stocks are held. In fact, many companies issue out a large portion of their shares as common shares.

Going by the features of common stocks, investors may prefer this kind of stock because they offer a higher return on investment. It may also be because they confer voting right. However, the risks attached to common stocks are higher when compared to corporate bonds and as such may be unattractive to risk-averse investors.

Preference shares

From the qualifier "preference," we can infer that this kind of share comes along with some, if you like, preferential treatment. Let's see if this is true.

Preference or preferred stocks (as it is sometimes called) has some features similar to those of bonds. One of them is that it does not confer voting rights on the holder.

In order words, the holder of preferred shares does not have the right to vote on who makes the board of directors. He has to depend on the decision made by the common shareholders in this regard.

It is, however, important to note that it is not a sacrosanct feature in a sense. While it is common practice in many companies to exempt preference shareholders from exercising voting rights, a few companies still allow them to. You may watch out for them if you intend to buy preference shares and still have a say in decisions.

In addition, preference shareholders necessarily (or at least in most cases) receive dividends. These dividends are usually fixed and they are regular.

This is a clear point on which preference shares differ from common shares. In some companies, common shareholders are totally ruled out of receiving dividends. However, when it comes to preference shares, their dividends have to be paid them.

As earlier noted, when a company goes bankrupt, it first settles the preference shareholders. Before ever common shareholders will be compensated, the holders of preference share would have been cleared.

In a sense, preference shares are somewhere between bonds and common shares. This means they share some features with both bonds and common stocks but belong to neither category.

An example would be that it pays part of its profits as dividends. Common shareholders equally have a right to such dividends. As pertaining to bonds, it does not confer voting rights (at least, most of the time). This is a typical feature of bonds.

Types of preference shares

Now, preference shares come in various shapes and sizes (permit me to use that phrase). There are cumulative and non-cumulative preference shares. There are also redeemable and irredeemable preference shares. There are also shares with the "callable" options.

Explaining the **callable preference shares**, it gives the issuer (that is, the company), the option of buying back the preference shares at a given price. In other words, the company who issues preference shares with the callable option can buy back those shares. This is however done paying a premium to the holders.

The cumulative preference shares obligates the company to accumulate the dividends for a later time when it cannot pay as at when due. This happens when the firm cannot pay up the dividends at the normal time. It may be lacking the resources to pay and so, can accumulate such payments until it is able to offset them.

The non-cumulative preference shares do not confer this obligation on the company. It means that in the event where a company cannot meet up with the regular dividends payments, it does not necessarily have to accumulate it. The firm may or may not choose to make such payments at a later date.

Lastly, **redeemable shares** are preference shares that come with a maturity date. At this date, the firm must repay the initial amount that was invested into the business via the purchase of the shares. From this point onwards, all the giving of dividends ceases. The shareholder no longer receives dividends.

Redeemable preference shares are quite common. It is the kind of preference shares commonly purchased.

Irredeemable preference shares do not come with the option of repaying the initial amount to its holder. Actually, it does not come with a maturity date per say. This kind of shares is very similar to common stocks going by this particular feature of "no maturity date."

They are therefore called perpetual preferred shares.

So far...

Here is a summary of all that has been said concerning preference or preferred stock. They allow the holders lay claim to fixed dividends that have to be paid regularly. They do not confer voting rights. In the case of a company going bankrupt, the preference shareholders are settled before the common shareholders.

We have also seen that depending on the type of preference shares held; dividends can be cumulated or allowed to fly once resources are not available to offset payments. Furthermore, a preference shareholder can be entitled to receive his initial investment at the end of an agreed period.

Finally, the firm can have the right to repurchase the preference share at a premium if such share has the callable option.

The option to buy either preference or preferred shares would, therefore, depend on a number of factors. These factors are already clear from the whole discussion of the characteristics of each share.

Just to highlight the factors, they include; ones financial circumstance backed by financial objectives. They also bother on the level of risk tolerance that an investor or a potential investor has.

Arguably, another factor could be the amount of money available to be invested as well as one's marital status.

All in all, both preference stocks and common stocks gives one the right to claim part of a company's assets. It also means the holders can share in the profits of the firm.

If the investor is more risk-friendly, he can opt for common shares. The one who is rather risk neutral or averse would be better off sticking to preference shares. He can then select the kind of preference shares to purchase.

The one who has a lot of spare resources to invest can diversify and buy both types of shares. That way, he gets to enjoy the benefits from both and spread the risk. In other words, if the company where his common shares are held folds up, he can fall back to the returns from his preference shares.

Lastly, the investor with just enough income and a family to cater for may choose the preference share. He may also seek to buy the cumulative preference share which is equally redeemable. This way, he can plan on the fixed dividends that he receives and still have his initial capital intact upon maturity.

So, make your pick… the choice is all yours.

CHAPTER 3

THE BASICS OF STOCK TRADING

Let's begin by considering what an IPO means.

You may need to be familiar with this term. It comes up every now and then in discussions concerning stocks.

IPO means Initial Public Offering. When the term is used, it refers to stocks which are being issued for the very first time. It is usually done by a private company and is made open to the public.

An IPO is sometimes issued out by a smaller company that needs capital to expand. They are also issued by well-established firms that are privately owned but seek to be traded publicly.

When an IPO is about to be issued, a series of questions have to be asked and answered. These questions bother on what kind of security would be issued and at what price.

There are also questions on the amount that should be issued out in shares as well as the right time to storm the market with the offering.

All of these questions are thought through and answered by an underwriting firm. Underwriting is carried out by investment bankers. What they do is to help the company seeking to raise capital from investors. They act in the company's stead.

The company wishing to issue its IPO contacts the underwriting firm who does all the necessary assessments and then arrives at a good offering price. The firm also considers the risk of investments and prices that too.

All the activities of the firm are to ensure that they are a market for the new set of shares to be issued.

The Stock Market

Stock markets are meeting points for the purchase and sales of shares. A price is decided upon when the buyers and sellers meet or pool together their demand against the supply.

Formerly, stock markets used to be only physical meeting points but today, there is a virtual network of different computers that provide room for non-physical trade. The computers also perform the function of recording transactions made via this electronic means.

The stocks market is sometimes called the **secondary market**. Rightly so it should. This is because primarily, IPOs are neither initiated nor facilitated here.

The activities that dominate the stocks market are those between holders of existing stocks and potential buyers. Even corporations who have their names listed on the exchange do not necessarily buy or sell their own shares.

This means that buying stocks from the stocks market can be likened to buying from a current shareholder of a company. The same is true when you sell stocks on the exchange, you do so to an interested buyer and not the company who initially issued them.

The stock market is, therefore, a secondary market. There is also primary market for stocks. The secondary market is essentially where holders of existing securities sell to interested buyers. In order words, securities that are already in the ownership of an investor are put out for sale to any intending buyer.

Also important to note is that asides individuals who trade in existing stocks, banks also engage in stock market activities. This is simply to clear the air on who the participants in the stock exchange markets are.

A bank can give out an initial mortgage security to a customer. It can then go on to trade such security on the stock market. The activities of mortgage banks and its trading of mortgage securities were what gave rise to the global financial Crisis of 2008/2009. (Just some history to check out).

Hence, when the secondary market is mentioned in another discussion, just think stock markets!

It is also important to note that prices in the secondary market are not pre-determined. Rather, they arrived at the interplay of demand and supply forces.

This means that if the demand for the shares of a particular company goes up, the price may also rise as well. This increased demand may come about as a result of speculations that such company's stocks will increase value wise.

Investors are more likely to rush at stocks that send good signals, leading the price to rise. The flip situation can also happen. Companies may not be able to make significant earnings. They stocks begin to lose its attractiveness and then its price goes down as demand declines.

The examples of physical stock markets with an ever growing market include the stock exchange in New York, Bombay Stock exchange and the London Stock exchange. There are a host of others.

Primary markets

We have considered what an IPO means. Again, it means Initial Public Offering. It refers to the series of activities accompany the issuance of new shares usually by a private company to the public.

When the IPO is issued, and investors buy them directly from the issuer, then it is a primary transaction. By primary transaction, I mean that it takes place in the primary market.

Recall that we have equally established the role of investments bankers in the issuance of IPOs. To reiterate, they work as underwriters in order to facilitate and create a market for the new issues.

Therefore, in the primary market, the investment bank that did the underwriting of the IPO meets with the intending investor. The bank makes clear the terms and condition of the stocks to be issued. The intending buyer agrees to them if it suits him.

To put it differently, it is the underwriting firm hired by the issuing company that transacts in the primary market. The other transacting party is the potential investor.

After the sale of the stocks have been made, the company who issued the shares gets the proceeds. However, it has to pay the investment bank its administrative fees.

This is how the primary market operates. If after the new issues are bought and the buyers feel the need to sell their shares, they go on to the secondary market to do so. It is outside the jurisdiction of the primary market.

The prices in the primary market are not set in the same way as those in the secondary market. Here, they are set beforehand.

CHAPTER 4

FITTING IN THE DOTS
THE BULLS AND THE BEARS

Having a good grasp of what stocks are may be incomplete without knowing these concepts. The bull market and the bear markets are types of market that are a function of what investors think of prices. The pessimism or optimism of investors at a point in time determine what kind of market is in operation.

Please note that the bulls and bears market is not conceptualized the same way as the primary and secondary markets. In order words, it does not have to do with whether a new issue is up for sale or not.

Basically, the animal names that are used to name the markets are a way to describe what happens therein. We will see that in a bit.

The bulls market.

This primarily refers to the buying and selling of securities whose prices are rising. It may also be a situation where the prices have not risen but are expected to.

It is good not to forget that the bulls market is sometimes used to refer to the Stock market as a whole. The term can also be used to describe bonds.

What is most peculiar about the bulls market is the optimism that surrounds the air, so to speak. We would normally have a bulls market present when the economy has a good outlook. That is, the unemployment rate is low, and people easily find jobs to do.

The presence of low unemployment rates will mean demands are stable and predictable. If people can easily find jobs, then it means that demand for normal goods is likely to be rising in such economy.

All things being equal, companies can maintain and even expand sales. Higher sales would translate into higher profits. Higher profits will push up the value of the company. Price of its stock will increase.

Characteristics of the bulls market

• Confidence portrayed by investors

• High level of optimism

• There are positive expectations about having great business.

You can also describe an investor who is optimistic about prices as being bullish in nature.

Being bullish, however, comes at a cost. An investor might be too optimistic not to notice the downturn of economic activities. The stock prices will keep being overvalued. This can lead to unfavorable outcomes.

An example would be the global financial crises of 2008 due to the crash in housing prices.

The lesson to take out of this is, being optimistic is good. But you must keep your eyes and ears to the ground while expecting positive outcomes.

Now, over to the bears. Before I proceed, try to think of what a bear looks like. What are its main features? How does the bear differ from the bull?

The bears market

This is quite the opposite of the bulls market. It suggests a pessimistic view about stock prices.

Take this scenario to help to remember these concepts and not mix them up. Bears tend to swipe downwards when moving their paws. Bulls do the opposite. This a vivid way to explain both terms.

A bears market is, therefore, one that is characterized by falling prices. Investors are pessimistic usually due to the economic look of things. When stock prices are trending downwards, then we are in a bears market.

The characteristics of the bears market are the direct opposite of those of the bulls market. One thing that is key is that both markets are birthed out of the general economic outlook. Having a dominance of the bears or bulls market is really a function of what phase of economic cycle is at play.

In other words, we are more likely to have a bulls market during the period of economic expansion. The bears market comes to the fore as the economy experiences a contraction.

An example of the bears market is the general fall in stock prices that accompanied the Stagflation era which began in 1982.

Summarily, trading in stocks is more about speculations. You must remember that. Investors speculate based on current economic happenings, past experiences and future expectations.

Also worthy of mention is that different investors speculate in different directions. That explains why an investor is so keen on selling his shares while another is so keen on buying the same.

How are stocks actually valued?

In the stock market, prices are very volatile. Recall what has been said about how prices are set in the secondary market. It is done by the interplay of demand and supply forces.

If the demand outstrips supply, then the price of stocks will go up. The reverse would be the case when there are more people willing to sells their shares than there are to buy them up.

Basically, the earnings of a business affect how much value investors place on a company's shares.

I will provide you with a simple illustration of how the valuation of a company is done. The market capitalization figures are dividing through by the number of outstanding shares. This gives the price of each share.

If the market capitalization of a corporation is say, $2,000,000 and the amount of outstanding shares is $200,000, then the price per share will be $20. This is the basic way by which the price of a stock is valued.

In all, it takes a good eye for the best stocks, the listening ear for the most trivial information and a brave heart to bear the risks. With these, my bet is that you would have a smooth sail as a beginner. (Or at least, with only a few bumps!)

CONCLUSION

Thank you again for downloading this book!

I hope this book was able to help you gain mastery of the concept of stocks, its varying types, and features. I also hope you are now well groomed on what the bulls and bears markets mean. Surely, you can say a thing or two about what stocks are not.

Finally, if you enjoyed this book, then I'd like to ask you for a favor, would you be kind enough to leave a review for this book on Amazon? It'd be greatly appreciated.

Thank you and good luck!

Preview Of 'Momentum Stocks'

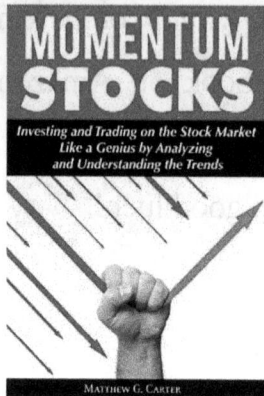

This book has actionable information on how to invest and trade on the stock market like a genius by analyzing and understanding the trends.

"The trend is your friend"

You've probably heard this saying before; of course it's one of the oldest sayings in the stock trading and investing world but what you might not know is that this saying is a shorter version of a longer sentence. The fuller version is actually *"The trend is your friend, until the end when it bends!"*

This full version affirms that there are two types of trend traders- those who follow the trend and make profits, and those who follow the trend, make profits and then lose it in the end.

Which of these traders do you want to be?

Trend trading is certainly a good thing- people like John. W. Henry earned millions of dollars from trend trading. From the proceeds of his investments, he bought the Boston Red Sox and the Liverpool Football Club and today, he is worth over $2.2billion.

The truth is that trend following is a very controversial topic; many financial advisors would advise you to stay off trend stocks, and that they don't work for stocks but people like John. W. Henry have proven them wrong.

People who tell you to stay off trend following simply have no idea about how to trade trend stocks; there are methods to these things ,and in this book, you're about to learn some of the secret strategies that successful trend traders use.

Check out the rest of '*Momentum Stocks: Investing and Trading on the Stock Market Like a Genius by Analyzing and Understanding the Trends*' on Amazon.

www.ingramcontent.com/pod-product-compliance
Lightning Source LLC
Chambersburg PA
CBHW071125210326
41519CB00020B/6423